CW00504433

Living in a Lifetime Home
A survey of residents' and developers' views

Leslie Sopp and Liz Wood

The **Joseph Rowntree Foundation** has supported this project as part of its programme of research and innovative development projects, which it hopes will be of value to policy makers and practitioners. The facts presented and views expressed in this report are, however, those of the authors and not necessarily those of the Foundation.

Research conducted by Consumers' Association and Liz Wood Associates
Commissioned by the Joseph Rowntree Foundation

Published for the Joseph Rowntree Foundation by YPS

ISBN 1 84263 018 0

Prepared and printed by:
York Publishing Services Ltd
64 Hallfield Road
Layerthorpe
York YO31 7ZQ
Tel: 01904 430033; Fax: 01904 430868; E-mail: orders@yps,ymn.co.uk

Contents

		Page
Acknowledgements		iv
1	**Introduction**	1
	Research objectives	1
2	**Executive summary**	4
	Overview	4
	The consumer perspective	4
	The trade perspective	6
3	**Main findings: the consumers' view**	8
	The Lifetime Home design features	8
	Likes and dislikes of the Lifetime Home	15
	Profile of the respondents	17
4	**Main findings: the professionals' view**	20
	Market status and trends	20
	Changes in regulations and planning	20
	Perspectives of the professionals involved	21
Notes		26
Appendix 1: Methodology		28
Appendix 2: The survey questionnaire		29
Appendix 3: Showcards		39
Appendix 4: The Lifetime Homes standards		42

Acknowledgements

We would like to thank the following organisations for their assistance in undertaking this study: Joseph Rowntree Housing Trust; Habinteg Housing Association; and the National House-Building Council (NHBC); along with (and not least) the residents and the professionals who contributed to the research. The interviewing for this study was managed by Total Research Services Ltd. Depth interviews were undertaken by Robert Ireland.

1 Introduction

Joseph Rowntree Foundation (JRF) commissioned Consumers' Association to carry out a study of Lifetime Homes, examining the views of residents and house-building professionals (builders, sales and letting agents).

To quote the JRF website information on Lifetime Homes:

In 1991 the Lifetime Homes concept was developed by a group of housing experts who came together as the Joseph Rowntree Foundation Lifetime Homes Group. Lifetime Homes have sixteen design features that ensure a new house or flat will meet the needs of most households. This does not mean that every family is surrounded by things that they do not need. The accent is on accessibility and design features that make the home flexible enough to meet whatever comes along in life: a teenager with a broken leg, a family member with serious illness, or parents carrying in heavy shopping and dealing with a pushchair.

The research programme aimed to provide an independent study to evaluate the desirability and acceptability of the specific Lifetime Home design features by consumers and to ascertain the current views of the private sector builders, sales staff and letting agents to the Part M initiatives and regulations.[1]

The research findings will enable the Joseph Rowntree Foundation to present empirical data and qualitative impressions of current perceptions and help shape views on how this initiative may develop in the future.

Research objectives

1 To undertake a large-scale study among existing Lifetime Home owners/renters:

- to obtain feedback from residents examining the importance or otherwise of the standards in deciding to rent/buy the property and whether or not these standards will be an important influence on future renting/purchasing decisions

- to establish consumer views on the design criteria themselves, from both a day-to-day context and also in relation to their physical needs.

- specific consumer questions that the research should address relate to establishing consumer attitudes and preferences concerning:

  - whether houses should or shouldn't have doorsteps
  - the balance between space used for hallways and corridors to improve access against reduced space in internal rooms, or whether a more open-plan environment is desirable
  - the value of a downstairs WC
  - the value of the opportunity to install a shower unit into a downstairs WC
  - the convenience or otherwise of sockets, switches and household controls
  - specific problems with any of the standards

- to identify the characteristics of households that find the criteria helpful/ desirable or otherwise

- to quantify the number of properties, and types of households, where subsequent adaptation has been made to the property, either to take the standards further, or to change the impact of the standards by reducing design features, etc.

Figure 1 The 16 design features of Lifetime Homes

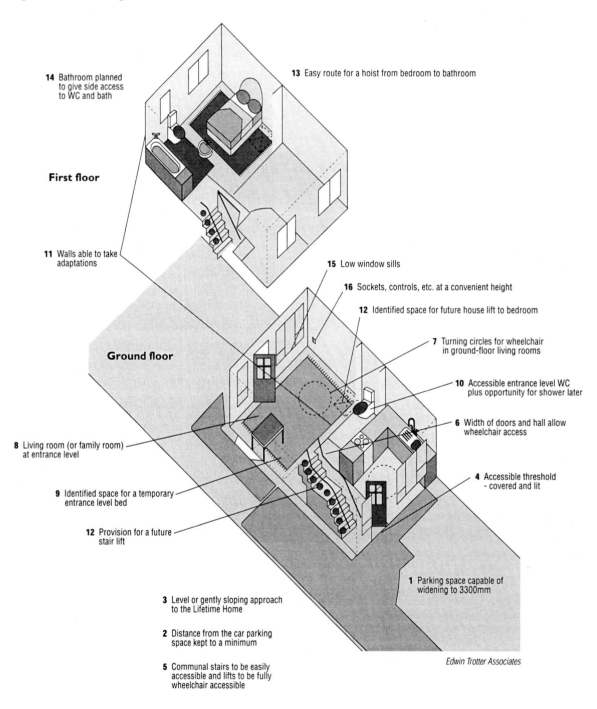

14 Bathroom planned to give side access to WC and bath

13 Easy route for a hoist from bedroom to bathroom

First floor

11 Walls able to take adaptations

15 Low window sills

16 Sockets, controls, etc. at a convenient height

12 Identified space for future house lift to bedroom

7 Turning circles for wheelchair in ground-floor living rooms

Ground floor

10 Accessible entrance level WC plus opportunity for shower later

6 Width of doors and hall allow wheelchair access

8 Living room (or family room) at entrance level

4 Accessible threshold - covered and lit

9 Identified space for a temporary entrance level bed

12 Provision for a future stair lift

1 Parking space capable of widening to 3300mm

3 Level or gently sloping approach to the Lifetime Home

2 Distance from the car parking space kept to a minimum

5 Communal stairs to be easily accessible and lifts to be fully wheelchair accessible

Edwin Trotter Associates

Note: Standard 5 on lifts and communal stairs applies only to flats

2

2   To undertake a small-scale research study among professionals involved in private sector building, letting and selling to establish their current attitudes and feelings about Part M specifications and Lifetime Homes.

Three-hundred-and-two residents in Lifetime Homes were interviewed face to face in their homes. The interviews with builders and other professionals were undertaken using a combination of face-to-face and telephone interviews. The research was undertaken between August and October 2000. The Lifetime Home residents were occupants of properties owned/built by The Joseph Rowntree Housing Trust (203 residents) or Habinteg Housing Association (99 residents).

The sample cannot, therefore, be taken as representative of either the general population or of *all* Lifetime Home residents (as we could not create a sampling frame of all Lifetime Home residents) but should, in our professional view, give a reasonably sound representation of the views of residents of Lifetime Homes.

The information collected in the interviews has been subjected to detailed analysis. Two main discriminating factors have emerged – age of resident and presence or absence of children. In some cases, the presence of a person with mobility problems does affect attitudes. Reference is made throughout the main findings where attitudes/experiences/needs, etc. differ between different groups. Further information on the methodology used in the study is appended.

In analysing the results of the survey, we have attempted to separate issues which are specific to a Lifetime Home from those that one would expect to be raised by a housing survey of this type, for example the perceived advantages of a smaller garden and easily maintained property amongst the more elderly residents compared with a larger house and garden for a growing family.

2 Executive summary

Overview

A survey was undertaken in Autumn 2000 to establish consumer views on the 16 Lifetime Home design standards including their perceived importance. The study also sought to identify the characteristics of households that find the design features of importance or not, and to quantify the number of properties, and types of households, where subsequent adaptations had been made to the property.

Two-hundred-and-three residents of Lifetime Homes built by Joseph Rowntree Housing Trust and 99 residents of Lifetime Homes built by Habinteg Housing Association were interviewed face to face in their homes. A small number of interviews with builders, sales and letting agents was also undertaken to establish the background attitudes to Lifetime Homes/Part M building regulations in the housing industry.

The survey showed that, whilst many residents were unaware that their home was a Lifetime Home, they thought that the concept was a good idea. Most had been able to move into their home without alterations being necessary beforehand.

The majority of residents viewed most of the 16 design standards as important. They were certainly of value to the broad spectrum of residents in this study. Whilst the residents interviewed were not representative of the general population, they included a broad age range, single parents, traditional families and retired people. Whilst some had disabled or physically disadvantaged/affected people in their household, many were all fit and well.

From the trade perspective, the introduction of Part M had not been as onerous as feared. It has, as expected, had an impact on costs but not to the extent that was anticipated. As far as the sales agents are concerned, they seem generally unaware that change has taken place.

The building industry has a sense of pride in having risen to the challenge and is now generally more concerned with other regulations (insulation and energy saving). The lack of adverse reaction from consumers, to date, may have been a major factor in damping down any backlash from the industry. It is possible that the impact of Part M has yet to be noticed by consumers (as many builders sought to get around the need to implement the changes on existing sites). This research suggests that consumers generally do not notice the changes, other than the access ramp. Some features, such as the large bathroom and downstairs toilet, are a positive attraction and benefit to most people.

The consumer perspective

The Lifetime Home design standards

The research was undertaken amongst residents of Lifetime Homes (LTH) but, as had been expected, many were unaware that their home would be classified as such and only half had heard the term before the interview took place. A quarter of LTH residents said that they were unaware of any special features in their home but almost two-thirds (64 per cent) spontaneously mentioned at least one of the LTH design standards. Wider doorways and the downstairs toilet (in houses/upstairs flats) were the most frequently mentioned. A third said that a special feature of their home was the wider hall and the same proportion spontaneously mentioned the easy-to-reach switches or sockets.

Table 1 Prompted awareness of Lifetime Home design features

		% aware
High level of awareness	Level/gently sloping entrance	99
	Covered front door with outside light	98
	Easy-to-reach switches/sockets, etc.	97
	Living room at entrance level	96
	Wider doorways	95
	Open space in downstairs rooms	92
	Accessible bathroom fittings	90
	Downstairs toilet with space for shower	88
	Car-parking space close to entrance	87
	Low-level, easy-to-open windows	86
Medium level of awareness	Space downstairs for a bed	67
	Strong walls in bathroom and toilet for grab rail	61
	Provision for house/stair lift	55
Low level of awareness	Extra wide parking space	41
	Removable wall panel for en-suite bathroom	31

Awareness of all of the design standards increased considerably on prompting but some features were less widely recognised than others, for example the removable wall panel and the extra wide parking space:

Residents generally valued the Lifetime Home design standards. Eight in ten thought that a car-parking space close to the entrance to their home was important, and six in ten viewed an extra wide parking space as important. Eight in ten said the covered entrance with outside light was important to them. A downstairs toilet was universally popular but only half thought it important to have the space and plumbing to install a shower in it.

Seven in ten said that the low-level, easy-to-open windows were important to them, as did three-quarters about the height of sockets, switches and controls.

Many people were unaware of the removable wall panel to make the bathroom en-suite and only a quarter thought this was important. Only a third of those in houses or upstairs flats thought the possibility of installing a lift from the ground floor was important.

Although around one in ten residents had reservations about the level approach to their front door or main entrance, six in ten would choose this over a step given the choice and a further three in ten had no preference.

Given the choice, a third said they would prefer narrower hallways and larger internal rooms, but three in ten would opt for the current arrangement of wider hallways and corridors and smaller internal rooms. However, a quarter would prefer a more open-plan arrangement. For residents, it is a question of balance between the benefits of spacious hallways for visitors, children to play in, turning buggies/wheelchairs, etc. against the limitations this places on space for furniture or to simply move around in living areas.

These residents clearly valued most of the design standards and eight in ten thought that the Lifetime Home concept was a good idea. Assuming that there was no difference in the cost, just over half would prefer to live in a Lifetime Home rather than a similar home without the design features (four in ten had no preference). Just over half would expect a Lifetime Home to cost about the same as a similar property without the design features but four in ten would expect it to cost more.

Lifetime Home residents

Although the sample of residents interviewed for the survey was by no means representative of the general population (or even all LTH residents), they included the full spectrum of ages from under 25 to over 75.

A third were under the age of 34 and three in ten were aged between 35 and 54. A third were employed in either full- or part-time jobs, three in ten were retired and around one in ten was permanently sick or disabled. Around half of the households had children or young people living there and half had a least one car.

Although the proportion of residents affected by some form of physical problem was higher than might be expected in the general population, the majority was fit and well as were the other members of their household.

Between one in five and a quarter of these homes were lived in, or regularly visited by, people with mobility problems. Fifteen per cent had someone living in the house or a regular visitor who used a wheelchair indoors increasing to 20 per cent for using a wheelchair when outdoors. Very few (7 per cent) residents or regular visitors used a walking frame either indoors or outdoors. Usage of a walking stick by

residents or regular visitors indoors was 24 per cent, increasing to 27 per cent when out of doors.

A third of those people interviewed said that they themselves were affected by a physical problem[1] increasing from only one in ten of the under-35s to six in ten amongst those aged 55 and over. The most widely experienced problem was moving around (climbing stairs, walking long distances or bending down) – this was prevalent among nine in ten of respondents with problems.

Having said this, only one in ten had needed to have any alterations done to the property before they could move in (generally a stair or floor lift or a shower).

The trade perspective

The introduction of Part M has had a significant impact on building practices and costs but not as much as was feared. The NHBC representative suggested that the industry took advantage of phased introduction to put off its implementation on sites for as long as possible.

Part M is hardest to accommodate in the lower-cost, smaller houses where margins are tighter and the amendments are likely to lead to a larger footprint. There is some suggestion that it is also problematic at the luxury end of the market.

Response to Part M

Sales agents seem to be generally unaware of the changes. Those who are selling new homes built to the revised specification seem to have encountered negative reactions from prospective purchasers only about the 'ramp'. The larger bathroom and downstairs toilet can be sold as a positive benefit.

Builders remain negative about Part M, although there appears to be little real hostility. It has been yet another obstacle to negotiate and is very much part of a trend of ever-tightening regulations and planning constraints.

Whilst there is no resistance to the principle of applying tight specifications to dedicated disabled housing, the main point of disagreement is with applying such regulations across all new homes.

The perception is that only a very small proportion of the purchasing public will positively benefit. It is suggested that some of the Part M specifications may be an active disadvantage for the able-bodied. Odd room-to-corridor proportions, outward-opening doors, etc. are likely to weigh in on the negative side.

However, the industry may concede that, for the most part, the changes are quite subtle and there is real doubt that the end user will even notice the design changes. Some of the specifications may have real benefit to a broader audience.

Builders and regulators have taken the regulations on board and are getting on with accommodating them. There has been little feedback from sales and the views of end users are unclear as only a few of the Part M specified homes have been sold. This should be followed up in further research if anecdotal feedback indicates consumer resistance or rejection.

Specific reservations

The main reservations are outlined below.

- Generally increased cost to the builder – building methods, redesign and pressure to increase house footprint (especially smaller homes) which translates as fewer houses on the site. This will inevitably lead to cost saving elsewhere or increasing the cost to the consumer (particularly undesirable in the case of starter homes).

- This type of specification further erodes builders' opportunity to design and specify according to their own judgement – creating an ever more homogenous and uninteresting end product.

- Whilst there are real benefits from ramps, they create considerable design problems (aesthetically poor, damp-course complications, very difficult on steeper sites).

- Downstairs WC is considered to be a luxury in the cheaper houses, which now have to be much larger. It is this that exerts most pressure to increase the house footprint.

The good news for Part M

The feedback from the industry is encouraging. There has been a change in attitude over the year and the industry has approached the challenge in a positive way. All admit that the reality has not been as onerous as they expected (in a sense they have weathered the storm).

The industry has succeeded in adapting in much the same way as it has had to with ventilation and thermal regulations. There is also a sense of pride and achievement as the redesign of homes may require ingenuity and creativity to accommodate all the regulations.

3 Main findings: the consumers' view

The Lifetime Home design features

Before exploring the individuals' views in detail, the level to which LTH residents were aware of existence of the design features was established.

Spontaneous awareness of the Lifetime Home design features[1]

Asked what, if any, special design features their home had, 11 per cent said that there were no special features and a further 15 per cent said they did not know of any. The proportion who were unaware of any special features in their home increased to four in ten amongst those aged under 35. Three in four interviewed gave what they believed to be specific design features.

A *wider doorway* was the most frequently mentioned feature (39 per cent). The spontaneous level of awareness of this feature was consistent across the different demographic and geographical groups.

Excluding the bungalow residents of Hartrigg Oaks, a third (35 per cent) of residents mentioned the *downstairs toilet*. The proportion mentioning this as a special feature of their home increased to 41 per cent amongst those with children in the household. Overall, 14 per cent said they had the provision for a *shower in the downstairs toilet*.

A quarter of the residents said that they had *easy-to-reach switches or sockets* in their home and one in ten said they had *low-level windows*.

A quarter spontaneously mentioned the *wider hall* and one in five the *wider stairs*. One in ten mentioned the provision for a *stair or house lift*. Sixteen per cent mentioned the *level or gently sloping approach* to their entrance, one in ten thought the *outside light* was a special design feature and the same proportion mentioned the *covered entrance*.

Prompted awareness of the Lifetime Home design features

Having been shown a list of the design features, residents were asked whether or not their home had each feature.

Car-parking provision

Most (87 per cent) said that they had a *car-parking space close to the entrance* to their home (92 per cent amongst the under-55s compared to 78 per cent amongst those aged 55 and over). Awareness of the *extra wide space* was much lower; only 41 per cent said that their home had this facility, 52 per cent said it did not and 7 per cent were unsure. Even where there was an adult with physical or mobility problems in the household, only 37 per cent were aware that they had an extra wide space.

The approach to the property

All but three people said they had a *level or gently sloping approach* to their home and all but four people recognised that they had a covered front door with outside light.

Internal layout

Almost all (95 per cent) said they had *wider doorways* in their home and 92 per cent were aware that they had *open space in their downstairs rooms* to turn wheelchairs/buggies, etc. Ninety-six per cent had a *living room at entrance level*.

Other features

Most people (88 per cent) said that they had a *downstairs toilet with space for a shower* to be installed.

Only 61 per cent were aware that they had *extra strong walls in bathroom and toilets* to fix grab rails but this depended very much on age, ranging from only 45 per cent amongst the under-35s to 88 per cent amongst those aged 55 and over. Awareness of the *removable wall panel* to make the bathroom en-suite was even lower (31 per cent), although it did increase to 48 per cent amongst the over-54s.

Ninety per cent said that their home had *taps that were easy to reach and turn on*, that is, lever rather than twist fittings (the definition used in the research to describe the accessible bathroom fittings standard). A small number of respondents had changed the bath or sink taps (see section on 'Adaptations to the property' later in this chapter).[2]

Amongst those living in houses or upstairs flats, 65 per cent were aware of the provision for a *house or stair lift*.

Only two-thirds thought they had *space downstairs for a bed* (57 per cent amongst the under-55s, but 85 per cent amongst those aged 55 and over).

Most (86 per cent) said they had *low-level, easy-to-open windows* and almost all (97 per cent) said they had *easy-to-reach sockets and switches*, etc.

Attitudes to the different design features
The value of the parking provisions
Eight in ten thought that a car-parking space close to the entrance to their home was important (half thought it very important). Six in ten had had space to park a car at their previous home (increasing to 85 per cent amongst those aged 55 and over) but this made no difference to the perceived importance for the current property. Not surprisingly, almost all

(94 per cent) of those people with at least one car in the household (53 per cent of those interviewed) said a parking space close to their home was important but, even amongst those without a car, two-thirds rated this as important.

There was also general support for an extra wide space in which to park the car, with 30 per cent saying this was very important and a further 28 per cent rating it fairly important.

The approach to the front door or main entrance
If they had the choice, 61 per cent would choose a level approach to their front door or main entrance, 9 per cent would prefer a step and 29 per cent did not have a preference.

Under the age of 55, around half would choose a level approach with most of the others having no preference. Over the age of 55, there was a clear preference for the level approach (75 per cent) with just 6 per cent choosing a step. Where there was an adult or child with physical problems in the household, the balance was also firmly in favour of a level approach. In households without someone affected by physical problems, 49 per cent elected for a level approach and 41 per cent of respondents said they had no preference.

The minority who would prefer a step generally said that this was to stop rain, insects, leaves, etc. from getting in under the door and to avoid the danger of flooding.

Support for the level access was due to a combination of factors; that it was good or necessary for wheelchair users, that it was easier for those with small children/buggies or simply that it made access easier. One in five said that steps could become a nuisance, a problem or even a danger with increasing age. Even where people favoured the level approach, there were still some concerns about the potential ingress of rain, etc. under the door.

The value of a covered entrance with outside light

This aspect of the design criteria was widely appreciated with eight in ten considering it important (55 per cent said it was very important to them). Amongst the older residents, 88 per cent said that this was important to them. Women were more likely to rate this as very important (59 per cent) than men (46 per cent). Single parents also attached higher importance to this feature (67 per cent said it was very important).

Internal design

Lifetime Home occupants were asked about their preferred balance between hallways and corridors to improve access against reduced space in internal rooms. They were asked which of the following three options they would choose if they could:

- wider hallways and corridors and smaller internal rooms

- narrower hallways and corridors and larger internal rooms

- open plan with few or no corridors.

There was support for all three options with slightly more people choosing the narrower hallways and larger internal rooms (36 per cent) than the existing arrangement of wider hallways and smaller internal rooms (27 per cent) or an open-plan arrangement (24 per cent). Preferences varied by age as shown in Table 2.

There were also corresponding variations by location with nearly half (46 per cent) of the residents of Hartrigg Oaks choosing narrower hallways and corridors and larger internal rooms, and only 8 per cent preferring wider hallways and corridors with smaller internal rooms.

In the other JRHT properties, 30 per cent chose narrower hallways and corridors and larger internal rooms, but 44 per cent preferred wider hallways and corridors with smaller internal rooms.

A quarter said they would prefer an open-plan design with few or no corridors. Those with children were significantly more likely (32 per cent) to choose this option than residents with no children in the household (16 per cent).

Table 2 If you had the choice, which would you prefer ...?

| | Age of respondent | | |
	All %	Under 35 %	35–54 %	55 and over %
Narrower hallways and corridors, larger internal rooms	36	36	30	40
Wider hallways and corridors, smaller internal rooms	27	25	37	22
Open plan with few or no corridors	24	32	27	12
Wider hallways and larger internal rooms	2	2	1	4
Total responding	**302**	**108**	**89**	**105**

The overwhelming reason was that it would feel more spacious or make better use of the space.

The choice of narrower hall and corridors with larger internal rooms was made on the basis that the occupant would prefer more living space/a bigger lounge. Those choosing a wider hall and corridors with smaller internal rooms felt that this option would be better for access and moving around, and would give more room for buggies and wheelchairs.

The results should be treated with some caution as many people seemed to be choosing what they believed was their current design (a quarter made their choice because they like the arrangement as it is now). However, some were clearly mistaken as to what the present design was, as shown in Table 3.

The value of a downstairs toilet
Amongst those living in properties on more than one level (i.e. excluding those in flats and bungalows), a downstairs toilet was considered by almost everyone to be important. Six in ten had a toilet on the entrance level in their previous home (increasing to seven in ten amongst those aged 55 and over). The proportion who considered a downstairs toilet to be very important increased from 63 per cent amongst the under-35s to 81 per cent amongst respondents aged 55 and over.

The value of the opportunity to install a shower unit in a downstairs toilet
Around half thought it important to have the space and plumbing to install a shower in the downstairs toilet. Again, older respondents placed greater importance on this than younger

Table 3 Reason for choice on internal design

Option chosen	Wider hallways and corridors, smaller internal rooms %	Narrower hallways and corridors, larger internal rooms %	Open plan with few or no corridors %
Like it as it is now	39	19	–
More spacious/more space/better use of space	12	15	61
Rather have more living space /bigger lounge	4	44	17
Better access/for moving around /for children visitors	20	12	21
More room for buggy/wheelchair	30	5	10
Easier to arrange furniture	–	7	3
Bigger kitchen	–	8	–
Let in more light/more light and airy	–	–	11
Like a large hall	8	–	–
Other	6	6	11
Total choosing	**83**	**108**	**72**

ones (48 per cent of the over-54s said it was very important to them).

The value of a removable wall panel to make the bathroom en-suite

This was an aspect that many were unaware of in their home and only a quarter (24 per cent) thought it important. Sixty-three per cent said that this was not important to them whilst 11 per cent had no preference. There was a marked difference in views across the age groups with 35 per cent of respondents aged 55 and over considering it important compared to just 17 per cent of the other residents. Consequently, those with no children in the household were more likely to consider it important (29 per cent) than those with children (17 per cent).

Low-level, easy-to-open windows

Seventy-one per cent said that this design feature was important to them. The level of importance increased with age from 55 per cent amongst the under-35s to 92 per cent amongst respondents aged 55 and over. Those with children in the household were less likely to consider this feature important (58 per cent) than those without children (84 per cent). In households where there was at least one adult with physical problems, 84 per cent said such windows were important (this compared with 63 per cent in households where all were able bodied).

Eighteen per cent of those with children in the household had installed childproof locks on the windows. This may or may not be a direct response to these types of windows in Lifetime Homes. We have not surveyed owners of non-Lifetime Homes to see whether households with children are any more or less likely to install childproof locks on windows.

The convenience or otherwise of sockets, switches and control heights

Three-quarters said that this was important to them (half said it was very important). Again, there was a marked age effect with 84 per cent of those aged over 54 saying this was very important compared to only 23 per cent amongst the under-35s (93 per cent and 60 per cent respectively considered this of importance to some extent).

Respondents with children in the household were less likely to consider this feature important (64 per cent) than those without (90 per cent). In households where there was at least one adult with physical problems, 89 per cent said this was important (this compares with 69 per cent in households where all were able bodied).

One in three (35 per cent) of those with children under ten years old in the household had put childproof safety covers on wall sockets. Again, just because the sockets happen to be located more visibly at mid-height rather than skirting-board level does not mean that putting socket covers on is specific to Lifetime Home residents – households with young children may be more likely to use socket covers regardless of their location or type of property.

The possibility of installing a lift from the ground floor to first floor

Views about this design criterion were very mixed. Overall, 31 per cent thought it important but 65 per cent took the opposite view. Opinions were age related, with only 17 per cent of the under-35s thinking this important compared to 70 per cent amongst the over-54s.[3] Six in ten of those with at least one physically affected adult in the household said this was important to them but, perhaps surprisingly, 37 per cent said it was not important. None of the few respondents with physically affected children thought it important.

Awareness of, and attitudes to, the Lifetime Home concept

Awareness of Lifetime Homes

Everyone interviewed in the survey lived in a Lifetime Home but only half said they had heard of the term before the interview. Although slightly fewer of those aged 55 and over (38 per cent) had heard the term, there was no particular pattern across the age groups.

Mainly due to the lower awareness amongst older respondents, those in households with at least one adult affected by physical problems were less likely to have heard of the term (43 per cent) than those with an able-bodied household (53 per cent).

Awareness levels varied according to location. Amongst residents in Joseph Rowntree Housing Trust (JRHT) properties other than Hartrigg Oaks, 68 per cent had heard of Lifetime Homes. Awareness levels amongst residents in the Habinteg properties ranged from just 14 per cent in Newcastle-upon-Tyne to 80 per cent in Bradford.

Only a very few respondents (3 per cent) said their previous home was a Lifetime Home.

Attitudes to the Lifetime Home concept

Most people thought that the idea behind Lifetime Homes was a good one (83 per cent) with only a small minority (3 per cent) thinking it a bad idea. The level of support for the idea was broadly consistent across the different age groups and there was no difference between the views of those with a disabled child or adult in the household and those without.

The importance of the design features for housing choice

Given the choice, and assuming that there was no difference in the cost, just over half (54 per cent) said they would prefer to live in a Lifetime Home with the design features that they had been shown. Only a small proportion (4 per cent) said they would prefer a similar property without the design features. Four in ten had no preference.

The likelihood to prefer to live in a Lifetime Home increased with age from 36 per cent amongst the under-35s to 77 per cent amongst those aged 55 and over. Amongst those who had at least one adult with physical problems, the preference for a Lifetime Home increased to 72 per cent. Three-quarters of those who were personally affected would prefer to live in a Lifetime Home. Where none of the household had any problems or disabilities, four in ten would prefer a Lifetime Home and half had no preference.

Women were more likely (56 per cent) to say they would prefer a Lifetime Home than men (47 per cent), who were as likely to have no preference (48 per cent).

Even where the present home does not meet their needs as well as their previous home did, the majority (67 per cent) would prefer to live in a Lifetime Home.

The preference for a Lifetime Home was sometimes due to an appreciation of the concept that they would not have to move house if their circumstances altered in the future (27 per cent):

I like the idea of staying for a lifetime. (Female, aged 27)

Looking to the future. (Female, aged 55–64)

You never know what's around the corner and could need to use the features in the future. I wouldn't have to move to have the house altered. (Female, aged 24)

Others said that the Lifetime Home meets their needs/that they need some or all of the design features (23 per cent) or simply like the design features (15 per cent):

Independent living only possible because of design features.
(Newcastle, two disabled people sharing)

Easy to get around the house – everything is accessible. (Female, 65)

Prefer wider doors and other features. (Female, 79)

Because of disabled facilities. (Male, 33)

Much easier to live with mobility problems. (Male, 74)

I'm getting older and it will meet my needs. (Female, 82)

Just over half (53 per cent) would expect a Lifetime Home to cost about the same as a similar property without the design features, but 39 per cent thought it would cost more.

Adaptations to the property

Only one in ten had needed to have any alterations done to the property before they could move in (slightly higher than the 7 per cent whose previous home had been altered in some way).

Three-quarters of respondents who had needed to have alterations made had at least one adult in the household with physical problems and 10 per cent had a child affected in some way. However, even where there was someone with physical problems (adult or child), eight in ten had been able to move into their Lifetime Home without alterations being necessary.

Most (71 per cent) of those people whose Lifetime Home had needed some alteration before they could move in were aged 55 or over but a quarter were aged 35–54.

The most frequent alteration was to install a stair or floor lift (23 per cent) followed by the installation of a shower (16 per cent). Thirteen per cent of those whose home had been altered said that their loft had been converted – all of these properties were at Hartrigg Oaks.

The pilot survey indicated (through both discussion and observation) that occupants had made changes to their homes, which did not fall into the category of 'alterations' as far as they were concerned. In the main survey, residents were given a list of changes that they might have made as a basis for discussion. Overall, 65 per cent said they had not made any changes but the results highlighted some interesting patterns.

Those people with children in the household were significantly more likely (44 per cent) to have made changes than those without (25 per cent). Top of the list was childproof safety covers on wall sockets; 16 per cent across the total sample but rising to 35 per cent of those with at least one child under ten (31 per cent of all those with children in the household). One in five of those with children (and the same proportion of those with under-tens) had put childproof locks on windows (12 per cent across the total sample). Some (7 per cent) of those with children had changed the bath or sink taps (5 per cent of the total sample).

Other changes that had been made included different door handles (4 per cent), rails in bath/shower/toilet (2 per cent), a shower (2 per cent) and a bath-lift (2 per cent).

Likes and dislikes of the Lifetime Home

Generally, the respondents were living in two-bedroom (42 per cent) or three-bedroom (41 per cent) properties. The proportion living in one-bedroom homes increased from less than 10 per cent amongst those aged under 55 to 24 per cent amongst those aged 55 and over. A third of those who were the only occupant were living in a one-bedroom property.

Sixty per cent of the Lifetime Home residents interviewed said that living in this home had made a lot of difference to them and their family, and a further 20 per cent said it had made a little difference. One in five said it had made no difference (24 per cent of the under-54s compared to only 12 per cent of the over-54s).

The proportion who said it had made a lot of difference was lowest amongst the under-35s (56 per cent rising to 63 per cent amongst the over-35s). Those without children were more likely to say that it had made a lot of difference (64 per cent) than those with children (56 per cent). Amongst those with at least one adult with physical problems, 68 per cent said the home had made a lot of difference to them.

However, the aspects of the home that those people for whom a Lifetime Home has made a positive difference do *not* seem to relate to the design concept. They are more likely to be appreciative of having a bigger house (19 per cent) with more space (particularly those with children – 35 per cent). In some cases, this is their first home or offers them a 'new start' (9

per cent). The nice area/neighbours, etc. were mentioned by 9 per cent. Amongst those aged 55 and over, 21 per cent felt more secure/looked after and 17 per cent no longer have worries about the upkeep of a house. For older people, it had given them somewhere that is easier to manage (14 per cent), without stairs (14 per cent) and the opportunity to be part of a community (15 per cent). For the younger people, they had somewhere that was safe for the children (14 per cent) and room for their children/family (11 per cent).

Six in ten (62 per cent) feel that their present home meets their needs, and those of their family and friends, better than their previous home; one in five (21 per cent) said it was about the same. A similar proportion (17 per cent) said it did not meet their needs as well as their previous home.

The younger the person, the more likely he or she was to feel that their Lifetime Home meets their needs better than their previous home. The way in which people viewed their homes clearly depended on where they are in terms of life-stage.

Younger people welcomed the larger rooms, increased space and the new/modern home, whereas older residents felt that the smaller house and/or garden was easier for them to manage. It is also worth noting that 13 per cent of the under-35s had previously lived with their parents or family, so this may be their first home. One in ten who said the Lifetime Home met their needs better said it was easier for their disabled spouse/child/themselves to get about in.

Overall, 17 per cent said that their present home does not suit them as well as their previous one. This increases with age to 30 per cent amongst those aged 55 and over. The main criticism is that either the house or certain rooms are too small. The older people in this group were more likely to complain about a lack of room for visitors or small visitor bedrooms.

What residents particularly liked about their home

Whilst some of the things that were particularly liked related specifically to Lifetime Home design specifications, these were less frequently mentioned than more general likes.

A third liked the size of the house, the space available and the size/number of rooms. The area, the people or the neighbourhood appealed to 16 per cent of Lifetime Home residents. Some (12 per cent) liked their garden. Twelve per cent liked the design/layout and 6 per cent commended their home for its light/open aspect.

The downstairs toilet was a feature that was particularly appreciated by around one in ten (12 per cent). A few people (6 per cent) said they liked the fact that their home was a Lifetime Home or was built for disabled/wheelchair access (increasing to 14 per cent where there was an adult with mobility problems in the household). A similar proportion spontaneously mentioned the wide doorways, corridors or stairs. Five per cent liked the large, or separate, bathroom and shower.

Possible improvements to the Lifetime Home

Thirteen per cent could not suggest any ways in which their home could be improved. The under-55s were more likely (17 per cent) to say nothing could be improved than older residents (6 per cent).

Overall, one in five (18 per cent) said that the rooms were too small or the wrong shape, often because of the effect that the downstairs toilet has on the size or shape of the living room:

Downstairs toilet takes lots of space from the living room.

None of the residents at Hartrigg Oaks mentioned this but a third of those in other JRHT properties did. Those with children were more likely to mention the size or shape of the rooms (22 per cent) than those without children.

One in ten (11 per cent) complained that the walls were too thin or that the soundproofing was inadequate. A similar number of people felt that the kitchen was too small. Again, this was more likely to be an issue amongst those with children (13 per cent) than amongst those without (6 per cent).

Amongst those aged 55 and over, the bath was a major area for improvement – a quarter of people in this age group complained that it was too low or the wrong size. All of these people were residents at Hartrigg Oaks where this is clearly a particular problem.

The window locks were another aspect which some thought could be improved. Overall, 6 per cent of residents mentioned this – all but one person being a JRHT resident. The residents at Hartrigg Oaks were more likely (19 per cent) to have a comment to make than other York residents (3 per cent). The elderly residents tended to find them difficult to use because they were too fiddly:

The window locks are very inconvenient and difficult.

Window fastening – the keys are quite ridiculous.

Difficult to lock windows – tiny key.

A few people expressed other concerns about the locks:

Door and window locks and catches are cheap and flimsy. The wooden frames are easy to break in.

It should also be noted that at least one 'creative' child in our sample properties was able to open the standard locks and extra locks had been necessary. This is unlikely to be typical though.

Some residents (6 per cent) complained that they could not get the car close enough to their door. Again, this was something mentioned by JRHT residents (often Alder Way, New Earswick) rather than those in Habinteg properties.

Six per cent of all residents thought that some aspect of the quality of building could be improved. Residents at the JRHT development at Woodlands, Acomb seem to have particular problems – more than half mentioned some aspect of build quality, for example poor quality fittings, unlevelled floors, noisy floorboards. The quality of windows and doors was subject to criticism from a number of residents:

Badly fitted windows and doors made of the wrong materials – wooden – warp and heavier with double-glazed glass panels. Could use PVC – low maintenance.

Double glazing poor – would prefer PVC.

Flimsy doors and windows – rattle and problems with condensation.

Difficult to replace doors – non-standard size.

Profile of the respondents

Age
The respondents covered the spectrum of ages from under 25 to over 75 (see Table 4).

Table 4 Age of the respondents

	%
16–24	5
25–34	30
35–44	20
45–54	10
55–64	4
65–75	14
75 and over	17

Gender
Seven in ten were female. The proportion of men taking part in the survey increased with age, from 22 per cent amongst the under-35s to 36 per cent of those aged 55 and over.

Employment status
Thirty-two per cent were employed in full- or part-time jobs, 30 per cent were retired, 17 per cent were looking after the home, 12 per cent were permanently sick or disabled, 5 per cent were unemployed and available for work, and 2 per cent were self-employed.

Home ownership
One in five of those interviewed owned their Lifetime Home. This increased to more than half amongst those aged 55 and over. Thirteen per cent had shared ownership and a few (2 per cent) had a lifetime lease. Six in ten were renting from a housing association, a proportion that increased to eight in ten amongst those aged under 55.

Type of property

This was defined by the interviewers undertaking the survey. Fifty-nine per cent were classified as semi-detached, 30 per cent terraced and 26 per cent as bungalows. Four per cent of those interviewed lived in ground-floor flats, 3 per cent in upstairs flats and 3 per cent in detached homes.

Length of residence

To be eligible for interview, the person must have lived in their Lifetime Home for at least six months. The following information should not, therefore, be taken as representative of all LTH occupiers.

Four in ten (37 per cent) had been in their home less than two years (increasing to over half amongst those aged over 54). Twenty-nine per cent had lived there for between two and four years, and 33 per cent for more than four years.

Car ownership

Details of car ownership are given in Table 5.

Table 5 Car ownership

	%
None	47
One	45
Two or more	7

Household composition

Forty-three per cent of those interviewed as part of the survey were the only adult in the household (rising from 31 per cent amongst the under-35s to 56 per cent of the over-54s). Half of the households had two adults.

Half (49 per cent) had children in the household (84 per cent amongst the under-35s falling to 63 per cent amongst those aged 35-54). Forty-two per cent of households had at least one child under the age of ten, 20 per cent had at least one child aged ten to 15 and 4 per cent at least one young person aged 16–17.

Seventeen per cent were single-parent households and 32 per cent could be defined as a traditional family (at least two adults plus children).

Physical problems

Very few said that either their regular visitors or the people living in the house used a walking frame indoors (6 per cent) or when out of doors (7 per cent). Slightly more used a wheelchair indoors (15 per cent) or when out of doors (20 per cent), or a walking stick indoors (24 per cent) or when out of doors (27 per cent).

A third of those taking part in the survey said that they had problems with at least one of the things listed on a card (see Appendix 3, Card F) which might affect the way people use or move around their home. The proportion experiencing such problems themselves increased from only 9 per cent amongst the under-35s to 63 per cent of those aged 55 and over. Sixteen per cent of those with children had problems as did 73 per cent of those with a child who was affected by problems. Eighty-eight per cent of those affected in some way had problems moving around, 43 per cent had difficulties reaching or stretching, 30 per cent personal care, 28 per cent dexterity, 24 per cent hearing, 12 per cent seeing and 6 per cent with continence.

In those households where there was more than one adult (57 per cent of the total sample), around one in five (22 per cent) had an adult other than the respondent who suffered from physical problems. This increased to 50 per cent amongst those aged 55 and over.

Ten per cent of the households with children (5 per cent of the total sample) had children in the household affected by physical problems.

Overall, 20 per cent said that at least one of their regular visitors is affected by physical problems. The younger the respondent, the more likely he or she was to have such visitors (25 per cent of the under-35s falling to 13 per cent amongst those aged 55 and over).

4 Main findings: the professionals' view

Market status and trends

It was clear from the qualitative interviews that there have been, and continue to be, significant shifts in the building industry. It is in constant evolution. The changes have been both good and bad.

On the positive side, the industry is growing:

They are building them and they are selling them.

There are greater profits to be made at the higher end of the market, which appears to some degree to fit with demands around some parts of the Birmingham area.[1] Brown-fill sites are a huge growth area in the major cities as people return to inner-city living and there are thought to have been general improvements in the design and build quality of new homes. These benefit both the end user and the industry:

* improvements in technology/techniques
* new regulations
* a move away from the homogenous boxes to more varied developments (more individualistic features)
* better materials
* increasing prefabrication
* higher specification of facilities (especially electrical).

The downside, from these professionals' point of view, is that planning and building regulations are becoming ever tighter, which could, at worst, strangle the industry. Procurement of development land is becoming increasingly difficult with less being available and constraints on how land can be developed.

There is fierce competition amongst builders.

The building industry can be seen as a growing but changing one where only the strongest and most responsive will flourish. Predictions are for continued opportunity but with ever tightening constraints.

Changes in regulations and planning

This is one of the main issues at the moment:

* ventilation – new regulations now fully absorbed by the industry
* thermal/energy conservation regulations – a major issue and one of the challenges of the moment (for some, on a par with Part M).

Most appear to be reasonably phlegmatic and accepting of the regulations, but there is real underlying concern that ever-tightening regulations are not always well advised and do not necessarily benefit either the consumer or the industry. They may serve to push prices up or choice and variety down as builders try to offset additional costs:

Costs have to be recovered somehow.

Attitudes to Part M

The strength of feeling regarding Part M varied quite considerably across this very small sample but the fundamental response was very consistent. The general view was that the benefits to the minority are outweighed by the cost to the industry and potential disadvantages to the able bodied:

An onerous requirement to apply to all new houses.

Builders do not pretend life wouldn't be easier without Part M but the industry prides itself on being responsive and market aware. They feel that they can make it work:

If you'd asked me if I'd rather not have had Part M, the answer would have been 'yes'.

Perspectives of the professionals involved

Sales agents

Sales agents are generally acutely aware of what customers want in a house but we had difficulty in finding agents who were aware of the Part M regulations, suggesting that this has had little impact on them (so far). The agent interviewed face to face said that local council rulings that a proportion of all new developments must be given over to affordable housing (housing associations, etc.) caused her some concern. She made no apologies for her observations that housing association tenants can lower the tone and reduce the desirability of adjoining properties.

Part M, on the other hand, seems to have had little impact. Sales agents felt that the initiative would benefit the elderly and disabled people who represent a minority of new home-buyers. Prospective purchasers seem to be largely unaware of any differences following Part M except for the 'ramp', which seems to be the only aspect that consumers ask about changing before completion:

Most do not notice the interior changes but younger couples tend not to like the ramp to the door.

The view of the agents who we spoke to was that consumers in the future will accept the changes as 'normal' and that:

... builders seem to accept new regulations as a matter of course.

Letting agents/housing associations

The depth interview was undertaken with a private letting agent who felt that he, and his colleagues, were less likely to be fully informed on building regulation changes as their job does not require this. They observe the broad housing changes but are insulated from the finer front-end details. Dealing mainly with older housing stock, the independent letting agent is unlikely to encounter Part M changes.

For the telephone interviews, we concentrated on housing associations. The interviews were conducted with personnel responsible for development. The associations built a combination of properties to Part M standards, LTH standards and also Scheme Development standards.

There was no evidence of problems from builders in responding to their construction requirements:

No problems with builders as more thought has to be put into the design of buildings so drawings tend to iron out any problems beforehand.

Although there was clearly support for the LTH principle, concerns were raised. The point was made that such homes are:

... not as marketable to younger people because of the look of the house ... and also that they do not think they will live there for a lifetime. (A view that we encountered in the consumer research)

Cost of build may also be an issue:

... in practice the larger floor area required means more expense so we need larger grants.

As far as housing associations are concerned, they will continue to build to required standards but may not be proactive in looking to change standards because they:

... do not have funds to implement new standards themselves.

Builders

Respondents from well-established, well-known building companies were interviewed covering the medium to large end of the house-building market. The companies involved in the telephone interviews were building both LTH and Part M standard homes.

Builders are generally very concerned with margins and fear that new regulations and legislation will cut into these. They approach costing as an equation where more constraints translate as less leeway for themselves and ultimately less choice for the consumer.

There seemed to be mixed views about the introduction of Part M. Whilst they may not have welcomed it, they could appreciate the intention behind it and have learned to live with it. However, there is still rejection of the logic of building all new homes to Part M specification when the proportion of the population who will actively benefit is so low. The application of blanket regulations can be seen to be counterproductive because different types of disability require different kinds of modifications:

Basically it's over the top.

A lot of new buyers are not disabled nor are any members of their family so they find the ramp a bit off-putting.

However:

Most new house buyers seem to accept the new regulations so it does not seem to have affected our business.

There were also some queries about the logic of some of the requirements. These tend to undermine confidence and trust in the regulations, a good example being the outward-opening bathroom doors, which are required downstairs but not upstairs.

In reality, applying Part M has been much less onerous than was anticipated. Adherence is now relatively painless for a number of reasons. There is a sense of satisfaction and pride at having successfully accommodated the new regulations – they have risen to the challenge. Most also admitted that the regulations are well laid out and easy to follow:

The lads in the drawing room had to think and the changes have been managed.

You overcome stuff once you get into it.

We are still on a learning curve.

It's simpler than you first think.

It has now become normal.

There is no doubt that the lack of negative reaction from consumers has helped the cause:

If you walked in you would probably never know.

I don't think the layperson would look if they weren't told.

Some of the requirements have a positive impact but there is also concern that buyers are being given a set of features that they don't want:

Everybody said, 'oh what a lovely big bathroom'.

They don't want ramps going to the front door or doors opening outwards into corridors.

A number of specific aspects were particularly contentious. These are dealt with below in the order of the perceived difficulty to accommodate them.

1   *Downstairs toilet.* This is not an issue for the larger houses where it is the convention, but has had huge impact on smaller properties (two beds or under) where this would not previously have been the norm. It adds to building costs, but, more importantly, means an increased footprint in developments where space is at a premium.

2   *Car parking.* This is also contentious and considered to be a real problem. The 3,300 mm width requirement significantly reduces the number of spaces available. The requirement for maximum distance from car park to the house also has a major impact on site layout and reduces spaces per site.

3   *Access ramps.* Often mentioned spontaneously (and referred to in this manner) when discussing Part M. They have a major impact aesthetically and are judged to be unattractive in many cases. They are one of the most visibly noticeable of the requirements, are difficult to accommodate on sloping sites and can create problems when trying to get damp-course levels right:

   .... the use of more engineering bricks above the damp course because of the ramp ...

makes the house less desirable to some people.

However, there is recognition of some universal practical advantages, for example the movement of heavy furniture in and out, and for dealing with pushchairs.

4   *Door width.* This can be rather cumbersome and, to the informed eye, may appear out of proportion.

5   *Light switch and socket heights.* Although there were some concerns about the positioning attracting the attention of children (which seems to be the case based on the consumer research), and the fact that the sockets might be rather unsightly, this was not a contentious change. The industry believes consumers will quickly accept the new design and:

   ... probably won't even notice.

6   *Corridor width.* Initially, a cause of concern, but new designs appear to have accommodated the change without great problem. There has been an impact on room proportions, but the consensus was that they are still acceptable.

7   *Level threshold.* Confirming the consumer research findings, the view amongst the builders was that this brings more benefits to customers than problems. However, on steeper sites, there may be a problem with surface water entering the house.

8   *Turnings spaces (foot and head of the stairs).* These had been accommodated with minimum difficulty.

The introduction of Part M has increased the cost to the builder. There has been the need to redesign all housing types to achieve the difficult balance of accommodating wider corridors and doorways without making the house disproportionate or increasing the footprint. Increasing the footprint will inevitably increase costs (fewer homes per site). This is particularly problematic in the smaller houses where the industry feels the real loser is going to be the end user:

It's immediately going to push up the price of new property because it will be a bigger area.

The reduction of the builder's scope to design what they want for the consumer could, at worst, encourage homogeneity.

The industry now seems to be firmly focused on regulations about energy saving – as with Part M, there are mixed views on this. Some respondents also mentioned timber-framed buildings as an issue for the future.

The NHBC

The NHBC likes to think of itself as impartial and tries to take a more measured view of the impact of Part M. Our respondent felt they had at least been consulted (unlike other industry sectors). He felt that the regulatory bodies (NHBC, etc) are able to take a wider view of the regulations as they understand the objectives better, whilst builders and developers are more likely to take a more parochial view, that is, how it will affect them.

In this respondent's view, the implementation of Part M has not been as bad as the expectation for two key reasons. First, there is built-in flexibility/leeway in all of the new regulations for special cases – they are no longer as prescriptive

as they used to be. Second, there is very little difference in desirability of a Part M specified house amongst the able bodied. None of the specifications are actually very radical or difficult to live with and some, such as the downstairs toilet and increased accessibility, are welcomed by most people:

In essence something of a trade-off – some minor irritations for some genuinely beneficial characteristics.

A measure of how well this respondent feels the industry has absorbed Part M is that, when it was introduced, builders were estimating it would increase the cost per house by up to £4,000. The reality after a year is an increase of approximately £1,000.

The way in which the change was introduced has caused problems for the regulators (NHBC and local authorities). Two criteria have been applied:

- any designs approved pre-June 1999 may be exempt, regardless of when construction began

- additional criteria that anything where construction had begun prior to October 1999, regardless of when approval was granted, is exempt from Part M.

There are three problems arising from this.

1 Developers tried to get around the regulations by applying for massive numbers of homes before the cut-off date.

2 Many sites were bought and foundations laid prior to the construction deadline.

3 On some sites, there are Part M specified homes right next to non-Part M specified

homes, which makes the job of inspections very complex.

The NHBC would have preferred a clean system where the cut-off was simply based on commencement of construction. In this way, there would have been much less scope for confusion.

The views expressed about the specific design standards tended to echo those of the builders and agents.

The downstairs toilet is particularly onerous in the smaller homes (two beds or less). It takes up too much space relative to the house size.

The access ramps are also a major point of contention and builders have been known to try to get around the regulations by making the rise from curtilage boundary to the entrance too steep for a ramp (after a given steepness, they can resort to traditional steps). The NHBC

representative suggested that much of the problem is with the language ('ramp' has connotations of ugly and industrial architecture whereas a 'graded approach' sounds much more sympathetic).

In this respondent's experience, the most acute problems occur at the cheap and very luxury end of the spectrum; the mid-ground size houses have little trouble accommodating Part M:

* cheaper equals smaller so accommodating different-sized spaces is difficult without increasing house footprint

* luxury usually means more individualistic and more discerning customers who strongly resent being told what is and what is not allowed.

Notes

Chapter 1

1 The Parts of the Building Regulations are as follows:

A   Structure
B   Fire safety
C   Site preparation and resistance to moisture
D   Toxic substances
E   Resistance to the passage of sound
F   Ventilation
G   Hygiene
H   Drainage and waste disposal
J   Heat-producing appliances
K   Protection from falling, collision and impact
L   Conservation of fuel and power
M   *Access and facilities for disabled people*
N   Glazing – safety in relation to impact, opening and cleaning
Reg. 7   Materials and workmanship
(Source: DETR).

The following is a description of the new Part M for Dwellings (provision for the disabled) (source: Barrow Borough Council):

Access and facilities for disabled people have been a core requirement of the Building Regulations for many years but have always excluded access to dwellings. From 25 October 1999 Part M of the Building Regulations will be extended to include access to new dwellings, including flats.

The requirement will apply if a dwelling is newly erected or has been substantially demolished leaving only the external walls. All future house designs must ensure that a disabled person can approach the principle storey of a dwelling, enter and circulate around it and have sanitary accommodation on that level.

Transitional provisions associated with these regulations introduce a further relevant date for consideration, that being 1 June 1999. These provisions indicate that:

- The new Part M will not apply to properties under construction on 25 October 1999, provided that the work began in accordance with a Building Notice/Deposited Plans and a commencement notice.

- The new Part M will apply to all new dwellings commenced after 25 October 1999 unless they are the subject of a full approval without conditions or a plans certificate obtained before 1 June 1999.

Chapter 2

1 A card was offered detailing things which could affect the way they used or moved about their home including: problems with moving around, difficulty reaching or stretching, dexterity, personal care, continence, hearing and seeing.

Chapter 3

1 The reported results are based on 273 interviews. Those for the Habinteg site in Newcastle have been excluded, as it would appear the interviewer presented the show card before (rather than after) asking this question.

2 In the pilot survey, one mother explained that, because of the position and type of tap

on the bath, it had sometimes caught in her sleeve when she was bathing her baby. Also, she found that her toddler could easily turn the taps on.

3 The results should be treated with some caution as only 20 respondents aged over 54 were asked for their views. The majority of interviewees in this age group were living in bungalows or ground-floor flats and the question was not of relevance to them.

Chapter 5

1 The depth interviews were conducted with builders, sales and letting agents in the West Midlands – see Appendix 1 for fuller description of the methodology and coverage.

Appendix 1: Methodology

Lifetime Home residents

Details of properties built to Lifetime Home design standards were provided by Riverside Housing Association, Habinteg Housing Association and Joseph Rowntree Housing Trust (JRHT). Notting Hill Home Ownership, Notting Hill Housing Trust and Maritime Housing Association were also approached but were unable to assist at the time.

As sponsor of the research, residents in Lifetime Homes built by JRHT accounted for two-thirds (203) of those interviewed. Residents in properties built by Habinteg Housing Association accounted for the other 99 interviews. We were unable to use the details provided by Riverside Housing Association for logistical reasons (they were very scattered geographically and there were too few at each location to make face-to-face interviewing a viable option).

All of the JRHT properties are built in or around York. It should be noted that a quarter of all interviews (72) were undertaken at Hartrigg Oaks, New Earswick – a Continuing Care Retirement Community completed in 1998. The 152 bungalows in the scheme are all built to LTH standards but are larger than the standard bungalows.

In addition to York, interviews were undertaken in Middlesbrough (ten), Newcastle-upon-Tyne (29), Bradford (ten), Hull (45) and London (eight).

Professionals

1 Five face-to-face interviews were conducted with parties active in the domestic housing industry in the Birmingham area:

- two home builders
  - one large (100–150 new homes per year)
  - one medium (approximately 60 new homes per year)
- one on-site sales agent – new homes
- one letting agent – new and older houses
- one NHBC representative.

2 Six semi-structured telephone interviews:

- representatives from two large house-builders:
  - one Construction Director
  - one Design Building Director
- two sales agents dealing with new homes:
  - one employed by a large house-builder (Midlands)
  - one working for a chain of estate agent (South East)
- two housing associations (Birmingham and Manchester):
  - one Senior Development Officer
  - one Head of Development.

Timing

All fieldwork was conducted between 19 September and 25 October 2000.

Appendix 2: The survey questionnaire

<table>
<tr><td>Joseph
Rowntree
Foundation</td><td>**Consumers'**
Association</td></tr>
</table>

My name is.................... **SHOW IDENTITY CARD**. I am working on behalf of the Joseph Rowntree Foundation, who have asked Consumers' Association to talk to people about their views on their home. **SHOW AUTHORITY LETTER IF NECESSARY.**

Q1. How long have you lived at this address? (2)

Less than 6 months	1 ⇨ CLOSE
More than 6 months but less than 2 years	2
2 to 4 years	3
More than 4 years	4
Don't know / can't remember	5

Q2a. And how long did you live at your previous address? (3)

Less than 6 months	1
More than 6 months but less than 2 years	2
2 to 4 years	3
More than 4 years	4
Don't know / can't remember	5

Q2b. Before talking about your home in more detail, I would like to ask you a few questions about where you lived before.
What type of house was it? (4)
CODE AS MANY AS APPLY e.g. A DETACHED BUNGALOW WOULD BE CODES 5 AND 7

Ground floor flat	1
Upstairs flat	2
Maisonette	3
Terrace house	4
Bungalow	5
Semi-detached	6
Detached	7

Other (please specify) _____

Q2c. Did you own it or rent it? (5)

Own	1
Rent	2

Q2d. How many bedrooms did you have there? [___] (6)

Q2e. And did you have.........

	Yes	No	
A toilet on the entrance level	1	2	(7)
Space to park a car	1	2	(8)

Q2f. Was your previous home altered in any way to suit the physical needs of either yourself or anyone else in your family? (9)

> Yes   1   ⇨   Q2g
> No   2   ⇨   Q3a

Q2g. What did these alterations involve? (10)

_____

_____

_____

_____

_____

Q3a. I'd now like to ask you some similar questions about your present home. How many bedrooms do you have here?

	(11)

Q3b. Did you need to have any alterations done before you could move in here? (12)

> Yes   1   ⇨   Q3c
> No   2   ⇨   Q4

Q3c. What did they involve? (13)

_____

_____

_____

_____

Q4. Having lived here for a while, what, if anything, do you particularly like about your home? PROBE IN DETAIL (14)

_____

_____

_____

_____

Q5. And what, if anything, do you think could be improved (15)

_____

_____

_____

_____

_____

Q6a. Does this home meet the needs of you, your family and visitors better, the same as or not as well as your previous home?   (16)

Better	1 ⇨ Q6b
Not as well	2 ⇨ Q6b
About the same	3 ⇨ Q7a

Q6b. In what way(s)? PROBE IN DETAIL   (17)

_____

_____

_____

_____

_____

Q7a What, if any, special design features does your home have?
DO NOT PROMPT

(18)

ENTRANCE
LEVEL OR GENTLY SLOPING APPROACH   1
COVERED ENTRANCE   2
OUTSIDE LIGHT   3
IN THE HOUSE
WIDER DOORWAYS   4
WIDER HALL   5
WIDER STAIRS   6
DOWNSTAIRS TOILET   7
PROVISION FOR SHOWER IN DOWNSTAIRS TOILET   8
PROVISION FOR STAIR / HOUSE LIFT   9
LOW LEVEL, EASY TO OPEN WINDOWS   10
EASY TO REACH ELECTRIC SOCKETS, SWITCHES, STOPCOCK,   11
METERS & MAINS SWITCH.

None   98
Don't know / can't remember   99

Other (write in) _____

Q7b **SHOWCARD A** Which, if any, of the things listed on this card does your home have? READ OUT EACH IN TURN AND CIRCLE CODE

	Yes	No	D/K	
1. EXTRA WIDE CAR PARKING SPACE	1	2	3	(19)
2. CAR PARKING SPACE CLOSE TO ENTRANCE	1	2	3	(20)
3. LEVEL OR GENTLY SLOPING APPROACH TO YOUR ENTRANCE (No steep slopes or steps)	1	2	3	(21)
4. COVERED FRONT DOOR WITH AN OUTSIDE LIGHT	1	2	3	(22)
5. WIDER DOORWAYS for wheelchair or baby buggy access	1	2	3	(23)
6. OPEN SPACE IN DOWNSTAIRS ROOMS to turn wheelchairs or baby buggies	1	2	3	(24)
7. DOWNSTAIRS TOILET with space for a shower to be installed if required and large enough for wheelchair users	1	2	3	(25)
8. LIVING ROOM AT ENTRANCE LEVEL	1	2	3	(26)
9. STRONG WALLS IN BATHROOM AND TOILETS TO FIX GRAB RAILS	1	2	3	(27)
10. SPACE DOWNSTAIRS FOR A BED	1	2	3	(28)
11. REMOVABLE WALL PANEL TO MAKE BATHROOM EN-SUITE	1	2	3	(29)
12. PROVISION FOR STAIR / HOUSE LIFT	1	2	3	(30)
13. ACCESSIBLE BATHROOM FITTINGS	1	2	3	(31)
14. LOW LEVEL, EASY TO OPEN WINDOWS	1	2	3	(32)
15. EASY TO REACH ELECTRIC SOCKETS, SWITCHES, STOPCOCK, METERS & MAINS SWITCH.	1	2	3	(33)
16. WIDE LIFTS TO ALL FLOORS IN BLOCKS OF FLATS suitable for wheelchair or baby buggy access	1	2	3	(34)

Q8. Have you heard of the term 'Lifetime Home'? (35)

Yes (mentioned spontaneously)	1
Yes (after prompting)	2
No	3

Q9. The idea behind Lifetime Homes is to design homes that are suitable for people of all ages and in different situations. A Lifetime Home would have the 16 design features listed on the card (SHOWCARD A). Lifetime Homes are intended to meet the needs of most households including those with young children and people with mobility problems.

Q9a. Do you think Lifetime Homes are a good or bad idea? (36)

A Good Idea	1
A Bad Idea	2
No views either way	3

Q10. I would now like to discuss some of the design features developed for Lifetime Homes in more detail.

Q10a. If you had the choice, would you prefer the approach to your front door or main entrance to be level or to have a step?

(37)

A step	1 ⇨ Q10b
Level	2 ⇨ Q10b
No preference	3 ⇨ Q11a

Q10b. Why is that? (38)

_____

_____

_____

_____

Q11a. Design standards 5, 6 and 7 on the card (SHOWCARD A) make it easier to move in and between rooms on the ground floor of a lifetime home but may mean that less space is available for the living areas.

If you had the choice, which of these options SHOWCARD B would you prefer? (39)

i)	Wider hallways and corridors and smaller internal rooms	1
ii)	narrower hallways and corridors and larger internal rooms	2
iii)	open plan with few or no corridors	3

Q11b. Why is that? (40)

_____

_____

_____

_____

_____

SHOWCARD C

Q12. ASK ALL **How important are each of the following to you?** RECORD ANSWERS IN GRID BELOW

	Very Important	Fairly important	Not very important	Not at all important	No Preference	
A car parking space close to the entrance to your home	1	2	3	4	5	(41)
An.extra wide space in which to park your car	1	2	3	4	5	(42)
A covered entrance with outside light	1	2	3	4	5	(43)
A removable wall panel to make the bathroom en-suite	1	2	3	4	5	(44)
Low level, easy to open windows	1	2	3	4	5	(45)
Easy to reach sockets and switches	1	2	3	4	5	(46)

Q13. IF PROPERTY IS ALL ON ONE LEVEL (e.g. A BUNGALOW) GO TO Q14a
ASK ALL LIVING IN A HOUSE OR PROPERTY ON MORE THAN ONE LEVEL **And how important are each of the following to you?**

	Very Important	Fairly important	Not very important	Not at all important	No Preference	
A downstairs toilet	1	2	3	4	5	(47)
The space and plumbing to put a shower unit in a downstairs toilet	1	2	3	4	5	(48)
The possibility of Installing a lift from ground to first floor	1	2	3	4	5	(49)

SHOWCARD D

Q14. **Some people have had to make changes in their homes to make living there easier or safer. Have you made any of the changes shown on the card or done anything similar?** INTERVIEWER REASSURE THAT INFORMATION WILL NOT BE GIVEN TO LANDLORD IF NECESSARY

(50)

None	1
Childproof locks on windows	2
Childproof safety covers on wall sockets	3
Different door handles	4
Different bath or sink taps	5
Intercom doorbell	6
Other (describe below)	

_____

_____

Q15a. Assuming that there was no difference in the cost, would you prefer to live in a Lifetime Home with the design features on the card or a similar property without them? (51)

        Lifetime Home   1 ⇨ Q15b
        Other Home   2 ⇨ Q15b
        No Preference   3 ⇨ Q16

Q15b. Why would you prefer that type of home? PROBE ON WHAT THE PERCEIVED ADVANTAGE OF ONE OVER THE OTHER IS (52)

_____

_____

_____

_____

_____

Q16. Would you expect a Lifetime Home to cost more, less or about the same as a similar property without the design features? (53)

        More   1
        Less   2
        About the same 3

Q17a. How much difference has living in this house made to you and your family? (54)

        A lot   1 ⇨ Q17b
        A Little   2 ⇨ Q17b
        None   3 ⇨ Q18

Q17b. In what way(s) has it made a difference? (55)

_____

_____

_____

_____

_____

Q18. Was your previous home a Lifetime Home? (56)

        Yes   1
        No   2
        Don't know   3

I now need to ask you some questions about yourself and any other people living here. Your answers will be treated in the strictest confidence.
SHOWCARD E
Q19. Which of these applies to your home situation?   (57)

Own: (Either paid for or buying on a mortgage).............   1
Shared ownership:..….   2
Renting from Housing Association   3
Other (write in) _____

Q20a. Do you, anyone else living here or any of your regular visitors ever.......

Use a wheelchair indoors	Yes	No	(58)
Use a wheelchair when out of doors	Yes	No	(59)
Use a walking frame indoors	Yes	No	(60)
Use a walking frame when out of doors	Yes	No	(61)
Use a walking stick indoors	Yes	No	(62)
Use a walking stick when out of doors	Yes	No	(63)

Q20b. SHOWCARD F On this card are a number of things which can affect the way in which people use or move around their home.
Do you have problems with any of these?   (64)

Yes   1 ⇨ Q20c
No   2 ⇨ Q21a

Q20c. Which code or codes on the card best describe your situation?(65)

CODE	
1	**Problems with moving around** such as Getting breathless climbing a flight of stairs, Difficulty climbing stairs Difficulty walking long distances Difficulty bending down to pull out a plug or to pick up the post
2	**Difficulty reaching or stretching** reaching up to kitchen cupboards or washing on the line
3	**Dexterity** – difficulty with picking things up, Turning taps or knobs
4	**Personal Care** – washing, dressing, eating, Getting in and out of bed or getting in and out of the bath
5	**Continence**
6	**Hearing**
7	**Seeing** difficulty reading the newspaper with your Glasses on

Other (write in) _____

_____

Q21a. Apart from yourself, how many adults aged 18 and over live in your household? (63)

None	5 ⇨ Q22a
One	1 ⇨ Q21b
Two	2 ⇨ Q21b
Three	3 ⇨ Q21b
Four or more	4 ⇨ Q21b

Q21b. SHOWCARD F Are any of the other adults living here affected by any of the things on the card? (64)

Yes 1
No 2

Q22a. Do you have any children or young people under the age of 18 living in your household? (65)

Yes 1 ⇨ Q22b
No 2 ⇨ Q23

Q22b. How many children are there in your household aged...
I) **under 10** RECORD BELOW,
II) **aged 10-15** RECORD BELOW
III) **aged 16 or 17?** RECORD BELOW

I) Children aged 0-9 (66)		II) Children aged 10-15 (67)		III) Children aged 16-17 (68)	
	1		1		1
	2		2		2
	3		3		3
4 or more	4	4 or more	4	4 or more	4
None	5	None	5	None	5

Q22c. Are any of the children living here affected by any of the things on the card? SHOWCARD F (69)

Yes 1
No 2

Q23. Are any of your regular visitors affected by any of the things on the card? SHOWCARD F (70)

Yes 1
No 2

Q24. What was your age last birthday? _____ (71)

16 - 24	1	55 - 64	5
25 - 34	2	65 - 75	6
35 - 44	3	76 +	7
45 - 54	4		

Q25. Working status head of household (72)

Employee in full or part time job   1
Self employed full or part-time 2
Full time education at school, college or university 3
Unemployed and available for work 4
Permanently sick/disabled 5
Wholly retired from work 6
Looking after the home   7
Other (write in)_____

Q26. How many cars do you have in the household? (73)

One	1
Two	2
Three or more	3
None	4

Respondent Name: Mr/Mrs/Miss/Ms

_____

Address:

_____

_____

Postcode _____ **Telephone no:**_____

THANK RESPONDENT & GIVE THEM A 'THANK YOU' LETTER

INTERVIEWER: PLEASE RECORD THE FOLLOWING INFORMATION BY
OBSERVATION OR FROM SAMPLE SHEET
Type of housing: CODE AS MANY AS APPLY e.g. A DETACHED
BUNGALOW WOULD BE CODES 5 AND 7 (74)

Ground floor flat   1
Upstairs flat   2
Maisonette   3
Terrace house   4
Bungalow   5
Semi-detached   6
Detached   7
Other (please specify) _____

Name of Developer: (75)
Joseph Rowntree Housing Trust.................. 1
Habinteg Housing Association...................... 2
Development Code (see contact sheet) _____ (76)
Interviewer declaration: I declare that this is an interview carried out in
accordance with your instructions with an informant unknown to me.

Signed _____

Date _____ / ____ / 2000

Appendix 3: Showcards

CARD A

CAR PARKING
1 EXTRA WIDE CAR PARKING SPACE

2 CAR PARKING SPACE CLOSE TO YOUR MAIN ENTRANCE

THE ENTRANCE
3 LEVEL OR GENTLY SLOPING APPROACH TO YOUR ENTRANCE (No steep slopes or steps)

4 COVERED FRONT DOOR WITH AN OUTSIDE LIGHT

IN THE HOUSE
5 WIDER DOORWAYS for wheelchair or baby buggy access

6 OPEN SPACE IN DOWNSTAIRS ROOMS to turn wheelchairs or baby buggies

7 DOWNSTAIRS TOILET with space for a shower to be installed if required and large enough for wheelchair users

8 LIVING ROOM AT ENTRANCE LEVEL

9 STRONG WALLS IN BATHROOM AND TOILETS TO FIX GRAB RAILS

10 SPACE DOWNSTAIRS FOR A BED

11 REMOVABLE WALL PANEL TO MAKE BATHROOM EN-SUITE

12 PROVISION FOR HOUSE LIFT

13 TAPS THAT ARE EASY TO REACH AND USE (Lever rather than twist to turn on)

14 LOW LEVEL, EASY TO OPEN WINDOWS

15 EASY TO REACH ELECTRIC SOCKETS, SWITCHES, STOPCOCK, METERS & MAIN SWITCH

IN BLOCKS OF FLATS
16 WIDE LIFTS TO ALL FLOORS suitable for wheelchair or baby buggy users

CARD B

1. Wider hallways and corridors and smaller internal rooms
2. Narrower hallways and corridors and larger internal rooms
3. Open plan with few or no corridors

CARD C

1. VERY IMPORTANT

2. FAIRLY IMPORTANT

3. NOT VERY IMPORTANT

4. NOT AT ALL IMPORTANT

CARD D

Childproof locks on windows
Childproof safety covers on wall sockets
Different door handles
Different bath or sink taps
Intercom doorbell

CARD E

1. OWN: (EITHER PAID FOR OR BUYING ON A MORTGAGE)

2. SHARED OWNERSHIP

3. RENTING FROM HOUSING ASSOCIATION

CARD F

CODE	
1	**Problems with moving around** such as Getting breathless climbing a flight of stairs, Difficulty climbing stairs Difficulty walking long distances Difficulty bending down to pull out a plug or to pick up the post
2	**Difficulty reaching or stretching** such as reaching up to kitchen cupboards or washing on the line
3	**Dexterity** – difficulty with picking things up, turning taps or knobs
4	**Personal Care** – difficulty with washing, dressing, eating, getting in and out of bed or getting in and out of the bath
5	**Continence**
6	**Hearing**
7	**Seeing** – difficulty reading the newspaper with your glasses on

Appendix 4: The Lifetime Homes standards

Table A4.1 sets out the full Lifetime Homes standards for reference. Homes that meet all the standards are entitled to be designated 'Lifetime Homes'. They will also meet the Part M Building Regulations, the relevant parts of the Housing Corporation Scheme Development Standards as indicated in the table, and the requirements of most local authorities for accessible housing.

Table A4.1 The Lifetime Homes Standards

Lifetime Homes standards	Specifications and dimensions which meet Lifetime Homes standards	Housing Corporation Scheme Development Standards compliance (E = essential, R = recommended)
1 Where there is car parking adjacent to the home, it should be capable of enlargement to attain 3,300 mm width	The general provision for a car parking space is 2,400 mm width. If an additional 900 mm width is not provided at the outset, there must be provision (e.g. a grass verge) for enlarging the overall width to 3,300 mm at a later date	1.1.3.4 E (requires actual provision at the outset rather than provision for later enlargement)
2 The distance from the car parking space to the home should be kept to a minimum and should be level or gently sloping	It is preferable to have a level approach. However, where the topography prevents this, a maximum gradient of 1: 12 is permissible on an individual slope of less than 5 metres or 1: 15 if it is between 5 and 10 m, and 1: 20 where it is more than 10 m. *Paths should be a minimum of 900 mm width	1.1.3.2 E (but covers natural surveillance, not distance)
3 The approach to all entrances should be level or gently sloping	See standard 2 above for the definition of gently sloping	Relevant parts of 1.3.1.1 E
4 All entrances should: (a) be illuminated relevant parts of 1.3.1.2 E b) have level access over the threshold and (c) have a covered main entrance	The threshold upstand should not exceed 15 mm	1.1.1.12 E

Table A4.1 The Lifetime Homes Standards (Cont.)

Lifetime Homes standards	Specifications and dimensions which meet Lifetime Homes standards		Housing Corporation Scheme Development Standards compliance (E = essential, R = recommended)
5 (a) Communal stairs should provide easy access and (b) where homes are reached by a lift, it should be fully wheelchair accessible	*Minimum dimensions for communal stairs* Uniform rise not more than 170 mm Uniform going not less than 250 mm Handrails extend 300 mm beyond top and bottom step Handrail height 900 mm from each nosing		1.4.1.5 E
	Minimum dimensions for lifts Clear landing entrances 1,500 x 1,500 mm Min. internal dimensions 1,100 x 1,400 mm Lift controls between 900 and 1,200 mm from the floor and 400 mm from the lift's internal front wall		1.2.1.44 E 1.2.1.45 E
6 The width of the doorways and hallways should conform to the specifications in the next column	*Doorway clear opening width (mm)* 750 or wider 750 775 900	*Corridor/passageway width (mm)* 900 (when approach is head-on) 1,200 (when approach is not head-on) 1,050 (when approach is not head-on) 900 (when approach is not head-on)	1.3.1.2 E 1.3.1.3 E 1.3.1.4 E
	The clear opening width of the front door should be 800 mm. There should be 300 mm to the side of the leading edge of doors on the entrance level		
7 There should be space for turning a wheelchair in dining areas and living rooms and adequate circulation space for wheelchair users elsewhere	A turning circle of 1,500 mm diameter or a 1,700 x 1,400 mm ellipse is required		1.3.1.12 R
8 The living room should be at entrance level			1.3.1.10 R

Table A4.1 The Lifetime Homes Standards (Cont.)

Lifetime Homes standards	Specifications and dimensions which meet Lifetime Homes standards	Housing Corporation Scheme Development Standards compliance (E = essential, R = recommended)
9 In houses of two or more storeys, there should be space on the entrance level that could be used as a convenient bed-space		1.6.3.6 R 1.3.1.11 R
10 There should be: (a) a wheelchair-accessible entrance level WC, with (b) drainage provision enabling a shower to be fitted in the future	The drainage provision for a future shower should be provided in all dwellings *Dwellings of three or more bedrooms* For dwellings with three or more bedrooms, or on one level, the WC must be fully accessible. A wheelchair user should be able to close the door from within the closet and achieve side transfer from a wheelchair to at least one side of the WC. There must be at least 1,100 mm clear space from the front of the WC bowl. The shower provision must be within the closet or adjacent to the closet (the WC could be an integral part of the bathroom in a flat or bungalow)** *Dwellings of two or fewer bedrooms* In small two-bedroom dwellings where the design has failed to achieve this fully accessible WC, the Part M standard WC will meet this standard	1.3.1.5 E 1.3.1.9 R 1.6.3.6 R
11 Walls in bathrooms and toilets should be capable of taking adaptations such as handrails	Wall reinforcements should be located between 300 and 1,500 mm from the floor	1.6.3.1 E
12 The design should incorporate: (a) provision for a future stair lift	There must be a minimum of 900 mm clear distance between the stair wall (on which the lift would normally be located) and the edge of the opposite handrail/balustrade.	1.3.1. 6 E 1.6.3.6 R

Table A4.1 The Lifetime Homes Standards (Cont.)

Lifetime Homes standards	Specifications and dimensions which meet Lifetime Homes standards	Housing Corporation Scheme Development Standards compliance (E = essential, R = recommended)
(b) a suitably identified space for a through-the-floor lift from the ground to the first floor, for example to a bedroom next to a bathroom	Unobstructed 'landings' are needed at top and bottom of stairs	
13 The design should provide for a reasonable route for a potential hoist from a main bedroom to the bathroom	Most timber trusses today are capable of taking a hoist and tracking. Technological advances in hoist design mean that a straight run is no longer a requirement	1.6.3.2 E 1.2.1.31 R
14 The bathroom should be designed to incorporate ease of access to the bath, WC and wash basin	Although there is not a requirement for a turning circle in bathrooms, sufficient space should be provided so that a wheelchair user could use the bathroom	
15 Living room window glazing should begin at 800 mm or lower and windows should be easy to open/operate	People should be able to see out of the window whilst seated. Wheelchair users should be able to operate at least one window in each room	1.4.1.1 E 1.2.1.32 R
16 Switches, sockets, ventilation and service controls should be at a height usable by all (i.e. between 450 and 1,200 mm from the floor)	This applies to all rooms including the kitchen and bathroom	1.3.1.14 R (switches, door handles and thermostats at 900–1,200 mm) 1.3.1.15 R (sockets at 450–600 mm)

Notes:
*Providing there are top, bottom and intermediate landings of not less than 1.2 m excluding the swing of doors and gates.
**But please note that it is important to meet the Part M dimensions specified to each side of the WC bowl in entrance level WCs (diagrams 10a and 10b). The Lifetime Homes standards for houses of three bedrooms or more require full side transfer from at least one side of the WC.

Source: JRF Lifetime Home website.